US MILITARY FORCES

MARINE CORPS

By Michael Portman

Gareth Stevens
Publishing

Please visit our website, www.garethstevens.com. For a free color catalog of all our high-quality books, call toll free 1-800-542-2595 or fax 1-877-542-2596.

Library of Congress Cataloging-in-Publication Data

Portman, Michael, 1976-
Marine Corps / Michael Portman.
    p. cm.— (US military forces)
Includes index.
ISBN 978-1-4339-5856-4 (pbk.)
ISBN 978-1-4339-5857-1 (6-pack)
ISBN 978-1-4339-5854-0 (library binding)
1. United States. Marine Corps—Juvenile literature. I. Title.
VE23.P67 2011
359.9'60973—dc22

2011004845

First Edition

Published in 2012 by
Gareth Stevens Publishing
111 East 14th Street, Suite 349
New York, NY 10003

Copyright © 2012 Gareth Stevens Publishing

Designer: Michael J. Flynn
Editor: Greg Roza

Photo credits: Cover, p. 1 Ian Hitchcock/Getty Images; p. 5 Lou Lowery/Archive Photos/Getty Images; pp. 6, 9, 22–23 (rifle), 24 Shutterstock.com; p. 7 Keystone-France/Gamma-Keystone/Getty Images; p. 8 U.S. Navy/Getty Images; p. 10 MPI/Archive Photos/Getty Images; p. 12 Buyenlarge/Archive Photos/Getty Images; p. 13 Dmitri Kessel/Time & Life Pictures/Getty Images; p. 15 Larry Burrows/Time & Life Pictures/Getty Images; p. 16 AFP/Getty Images; p. 17 David McNew/Getty Images; p. 18 Chris Hondros/Getty Images; pp. 20, 21 Scott Olson/Getty Images; pp. 22–23 (Abrams tank) U.S. Army/Getty Images; p. 25 Alex Wong/Getty Images; p. 26 Frederick M. Brown/Getty Images; p. 27 NASA/Getty Images; p. 29 Stan Honda/AFP/Getty Images.

Printed in the United States of America

CPSIA compliance information: Batch #CS11GS: For further information contact Gareth Stevens, New York, New York at 1-800-542-2595.

CONTENTS

Words in the glossary appear in **bold** type the first time they are used in the text.

THE FLAGS ON IWO JIMA

Toward the end of World War II, a US Marine Corps patrol had been given orders to capture the top of Mount Suribachi, the highest point on the island of Iwo Jima near Japan. In the distance, the marines could see smoke rising from the top of the volcano. The volcano was inactive, so the smoke could mean only one thing—Japanese soldiers were inside.

After the fifth day, the patrol reached the top without firing a single shot. Photographer Joe Rosenthal was on his way up to take pictures when he learned he was too late. The US flag had already been raised.

The Battle on Film

The Battle of Iwo Jima has been featured in numerous movies and television shows. Two recent examples are *Flags of Our Fathers* and *Letters from Iwo Jima*. *Flags of Our Fathers* tells the story of the marines who fought in the battle. *Letters from Iwo Jima* tells the story from the Japanese point of view.

The flag on Mount Suribachi—shown in this photograph taken by marine Lou Lowery—could not be seen clearly from the nearby beaches. So the marines put up a second, larger flag.

5

When Rosenthal reached the top, he saw that a group of marines was preparing to raise a larger flag to replace the first one. Quickly, he swung his camera up and snapped a picture.

The image that Rosenthal captured on February 23, 1945, became the most famous photograph of World War II and one of the most famous photographs in the world. Although the Battle of Iwo Jima lasted for another 31 days, Joe Rosenthal's photograph became a **symbol** of victory and courage. Today, that image still symbolizes the spirit of the US Marine Corps.

A Meaningful Moment

The picture of the second flag raising on Iwo Jima has been copied countless times. It served as a symbol for a 1945 fundraising drive that collected $26.3 billion for the war effort. The Marine Corps Memorial in Arlington, Virginia, was modeled after it.

Joe Rosenthal was awarded the 1945 Pulitzer Prize for Photography for his photo of the flag raising on Iwo Jima.

7

READY FOR ANYTHING

The Marine Corps, or just marines, is the smallest branch of the US military. The purpose of the Marine Corps is to quickly respond to any threat the United States faces, anywhere in the world. The marines must always be ready for any mission. Despite their small numbers, the marines have faced some of the biggest challenges in US military history.

Marines board a helicopter on a naval ship in the Indian Ocean to help deliver supplies to people affected by massive floods in Pakistan.

Many marine **units** are stationed on US Navy ships around the world. This makes it much easier for marines to enter combat rapidly. The marines and the navy have a close relationship that dates back to the American Revolutionary War.

The Eagle, Globe, and Anchor

The Eagle, Globe, and Anchor is the official **emblem** of the Marine Corps. The eagle represents the United States, the globe represents the marines' worldwide presence, and the anchor represents their naval history.

EARLY DAYS

The US Marine Corps was founded on November 10, 1775. The Continental Marines were a naval **infantry** created to fight the British during the American Revolutionary War. They provided security for naval vessels and led raids on British ships and forts. After the war, the Continental Marines came to an end.

Continental Marines on a navy ship prepare for a fight with Shawnee Indians on the Ohio River in 1782.

In 1798, the marines were reestablished to protect US ships from pirates near Africa. In 1805, the marines defeated the pirates at the Battle of Derna in Tripoli (today called Libya). It was the first overseas land battle the United States fought and the first time the American flag was raised in another country.

The "Marines' Hymn"

In 1847, during the US-Mexican War, the marines captured a castle known as the Halls of Montezuma. That victory and the Battle of Derna are remembered in the first line of the "Marines' Hymn": "From the Halls of Montezuma, to the shores of Tripoli, we fight our country's battles in the air, on land, and sea."

In World War I, the marines became known as tough and fearless fighters. Despite being outnumbered, they won the Battle of Belleau Wood in France. They earned the nickname "Devil Dogs," a name still used today.

In World War II, the Marine Corps played a major role in defeating the Japanese. Dozens of islands in the Pacific Ocean were controlled by Japanese forces. It was the marines' job to get control of the islands. To get ashore from the naval ships, the marines used small vehicles that could travel on both water and land. This **tactic** is called **amphibious** assault.

Join the U.S. Marine Corps. Soldiers of the Sea!

This poster from around 1914 shows a group of marines traveling bravely into battle on a small ship.

The marines used amphibious vehicles such as this one when capturing islands during World War II.

Island Hopping

During World War II, the United States captured key islands in the Pacific Ocean, one by one. Eventually, US bombers were able to reach Japan by flying from one island to another, which became known as island hopping. It was the job of the Marine Corps to capture these islands.

During the Korean War, the marines were called upon to recover South Korea's capital city of Seoul from the North Koreans. In what's known as the Inchon Landing, the marines used an amphibious assault to quickly land behind enemy lines and make their way towards Seoul. After 2 weeks, the North Korean army fled the city.

During the Vietnam War, the marines fought in many battles and successfully **defended** an important base. In 1989, they took part in a mission to capture Panamanian **dictator** Manuel Noriega. In 1991, during Operation Desert Storm, marine pilots destroyed Iraq's air and naval forces.

Fast Response

The Marine Prepositioning Force was created in 1986. It's made up of ships stationed around the world that contain all the supplies that marines would need for 30 days of combat. This allows the marines to begin operating in a distant country as quickly as possible.

Marines come
ashore in 1965
during the
Vietnam War.

WAR ON TERROR

On September 11, 2001, terrorists attacked New York City and Washington, DC. These events sparked the war on terror. The marines were **deployed** to Afghanistan in an effort to beat al-Qaeda and Taliban forces. On November 25, 2001, they quickly seized an important airstrip. This marked the beginning of the longest war in American history.

In 2003, marines were deployed to Iraq as part of Operation Iraqi Freedom. In addition to battling **insurgents**, they were responsible for security patrols and peacekeeping efforts. On January 23, 2010, the marines ended operations in Iraq. Their focus turned once again to Afghanistan.

In 2003, marines prepare to take over a hospital held by the Iraqi military in the city of Nasiriyah.

Marine Corps Camo

In 2002, the Marine Corps began using a new kind of computer-generated camouflage. The camouflage is made up of overlapping squares that make it hard to detect, even with hi-tech cameras and **scopes.** Since then, other military forces have begun using similar camouflage.

The Marine Corps is part of the Department of the Navy. Marine ranks are divided into three categories: commissioned officer, warrant officer, and **enlisted** soldier. Commissioned officers receive a formal document, or commission, from the president that gives them their rank and leadership duties.

The enlisted ranks make up the majority of the corps. An enlisted marine who reaches the rank of corporal is considered a noncommissioned officer. Warrant officers are noncommissioned officers who are experts with special equipment. To become a warrant officer, a marine must achieve the rank of sergeant.

Corpsmen

The marines don't train a medical corps. Instead, their medics are provided by the navy and are called corpsmen. Corpsmen wear marine uniforms with navy badges. One of the six flag raisers on Iwo Jima was a navy corpsman.

MARINE RANKS

Commissioned Officers	general
	lieutenant general
	major general
	brigadier general
	colonel
	lieutenant colonel
	major
	captain
	first lieutenant
	second lieutenant
Warrant Officers	chief warrant officer 5
	chief warrant officer 4
	chief warrant officer 3
	chief warrant officer 2
	warrant officer 1
Enlisted	sergeant major of the marine corps
	sergeant major
	master gunnery sergeant
	first sergeant
	master sergeant
	gunnery sergeant
	staff sergeant
	corporal
	lance corporal
	private first class
	private

TOUGH TRAINING

Marines go through a 12-week training process called boot camp. Boot camp teaches new **recruits** the skills and values of the Marine Corps. One of the most important skills is **marksmanship**. Every marine must be skilled with a rifle.

Becoming an officer requires a college degree. Then the marine must complete Officer Candidates School in Quantico, Virginia. After that, new officers spend 6 months in a place called the Basic School for further training and education. Then, they receive specialized training in their chosen field. Only then will an officer be given command of other marines.

A female recruit participates in urban warfare training during boot camp.

A Hard Journey

Marine Corps boot camp is considered one of the toughest in the world. Almost immediately after they arrive, new recruits must complete challenging physical fitness tests. The challenges get harder over the next 12 weeks.

Marine boot camp is held at the Marine Corps Recruit Depot in Parris Island, South Carolina, or San Diego, California.

MARINE CORPS GEAR

The Marine Corps uses many weapons—from simple knives to state-of-the-art fighter jets. A marine's most important weapon is the M16 rifle. Marines have used the M16 since the mid-1960s. An updated model called the M16A4 can be fitted with different scopes, laser sights, or even a grenade launcher.

Marines use a variety of vehicles, including the M1A1 Abrams tank, which is one of the most advanced tanks in the world. The AAV-7 Amphibious Assault Vehicle is made to carry marines on land and water. It's big enough to hold 24 marines or 10,000 pounds (4,540 kg) of equipment.

M1A1 Abrams tank

M16 rifle

The Higgins Boat

The Higgins Boat was the Marine Corps' first amphibious vehicle. It was invented by Andrew Higgins, a boatbuilder in New Orleans, Louisiana. It was widely used during World War II to carry troops and supplies from ship to shore.

AV-8B Harrier II

The AV-8B Harrier II is sometimes called a "jump jet" because of its ability to take off straight up.

The marines use aircraft to support ground forces during missions. Perhaps the most famous is the jet called the AV-8B Harrier II. Its engines can change position so that the jet can take off straight up and **hover** in midair. This allows the Harrier to be used in places that lack a runway.

The AH-1W Super Cobra is the marines' attack helicopter. It can be used in a variety of situations, both day and night, and in nearly any kind of weather. In 2011, a new and more powerful attack helicopter was added to the Marine Corps—the AH-1Z Viper.

Marine One and Marine Two

One of the duties of the Marine Corps is to provide helicopter transportation for the president and vice president of the United States. As soon as the president boards a helicopter, it's called Marine One. When the vice president boards a helicopter, it's called Marine Two.

Marine One, carrying President George W. Bush, lands on the South Lawn of the White House.

Some famous people were marines. Many American astronauts were marines, the most famous being John Glenn. John Glenn served as a fighter pilot in World War II and Korea. In 1962, he became the first American to orbit Earth. Former secretary of state James Baker and Robert Mueller, director of the FBI, also served in the marines.

Numerous professional athletes and celebrities have spent time in the marines. Ahmard Hall, fullback for the Tennessee Titans of the NFL, served in the marines from 1998 to 2002. Drew Carey, actor and host of the game show *The Price Is Right*, was a member of the Marines Corps **Reserve**.

Drew Carey

Navajo Code Talkers

During World War II, young marines who were Navajo Indians used their ancient language to create a secret code for messages. This method was both fast and secure, and impossible for the Japanese to decode. The Navajo code talkers saved thousands of American lives.

John Glenn poses in a space suit at Cape Canaveral, Florida, in 1962.

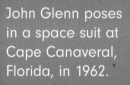

John Glenn

27

MODERN MISSIONS

The US Marine Corps was created as an amphibious force. Since September 11, 2001, marines have been heavily focused on fighting land wars in Afghanistan and Iraq. However, they continue to perform amphibious operations around the world. The Marine Corps doesn't just use its amphibious capabilities for combat; it also uses them to help people during natural **disasters**. Recently, marines have assisted victims of Hurricane Katrina, the 2010 earthquake in Haiti, and flooding in Pakistan.

Whether it's war or natural disaster, the US Marine Corps is always ready to respond on land, on water, and in the air.

Semper Fi!

The Marine Corps' motto is *Semper Fidelis*. These Latin words mean "always faithful." The motto was adopted by the marines in 1883. Often shortened to *Semper Fi*, it reminds marines to be faithful to the mission, each other, the corps, and the country.

In January 2010, marines deliver water to earthquake victims in Haiti.

GLOSSARY

amphibious: having to do with the capability to operate on both land and water

defend: to keep something safe during an attack

deploy: to move troops into a position of readiness

dictator: someone who rules a country by force

disaster: an event that causes much suffering or loss

emblem: a sign that represents a person or group

enlisted: members of the military who rank below commissioned or warrant officers

hover: to float in the air without moving around much

infantry: soldiers trained to fight on foot

insurgent: a person who takes part in a fight to overthrow authority

marksmanship: skill in shooting a gun or rifle

motto: a short saying that expresses a rule to live by

recruit: a new member of a military force

reserve: referring to soldiers who are not part of a country's main forces, but may be called to active duty in times of need

scope: a small telescope fitted onto a rifle

symbol: a picture or shape that stands for something else

tactic: a method for accomplishing a military goal

unit: a group of soldiers that is part of a larger whole

FOR MORE INFORMATION

Books

David, Jack. *United States Marine Corps*. Minneapolis, MN: Bellwether Media, 2008.

Kaelberer, Angie Peterson. *U.S. Marine Corps Assault Vehicles*. Mankato, MN: Capstone Press, 2007.

Montana, Jack. *Marines*. Broomall, PA: Mason Crest Publishers, 2011.

Websites

How the U.S. Marines Work
science.howstuffworks.com/marines.htm
Learn more about how the US Marine Corps works.

US Marine Corps
www.marines.com
Go to the official website of the US Marine Corps to learn more about this branch of the US military.

Publisher's note to educators and parents: Our editors have carefully reviewed these websites to ensure that they are suitable for students. Many websites change frequently, however, and we cannot guarantee that a site's future contents will continue to meet our high standards of quality and educational value. Be advised that students should be closely supervised whenever they access the Internet.

INDEX